READY, SET, GROW: ANIMALS

A DOG GROWS

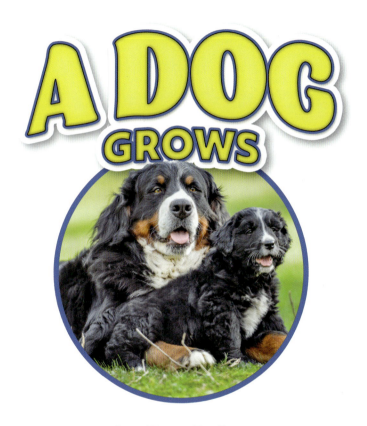

by Rex Ruby

Consultant: Beth Gambro,
Reading Specialist, Yorkville, Illinois

Minneapolis, Minnesota

Teaching Tips

Before Reading

- Look at the cover of the book. Discuss the picture and the title.

- Ask readers to brainstorm a list of what they already know about dogs. What can they expect to see in the book?

- Go on a picture walk, looking through the pictures to discuss vocabulary and make predictions about the text.

During Reading

- Read for purpose. Encourage readers to think about how a dog grows as they are reading.

- Ask readers to look for the details of the book. What are they learning about different stages of the growing process?

- If readers encounter an unknown word, ask them to look at the sounds in the word. Then, ask them to look at the rest of the page. Are there any clues to help them understand?

After Reading

- Encourage readers to pick a buddy and reread the book together.

- Ask readers to name two things that happen as a dog grows. Find the pages that tell about these things.

- Ask readers to write or draw something they learned about dogs.

Credits

Cover and title page, © iStock; 3 © smrm1977/Adobe Stock; 5, © ammitmedia/Adobe Stock; 7, © serova_ekaterina/Adobe Stock; 9, © Bearport Publishing; 10–11, © Bearport Publishing; 12, © Anna Hoychuk/Shutterstock; 13, © Anna Hoychuk/Shutterstock; 15, © Gladskikh Tatiana/Shutterstock; 17, © Anastasiia/Adobe Stock; 18–19, © Mdv Edwards/Adobe Stock; 21, © Alona Rjabceva Otsphoto/Adobe Stock; 22TR, © Okeanas/Adobe Stock; 22ML, © Eric Isselee/Shutterstock; 22BR, © Natallia Yaumenenka/Shutterstock; 23TL, © 5second/Adobe Stock; 23TR, © Bearport Publishing; 23BL, © dogphotos/Adobe Stock; 23BR, © Barna Tanko/Adobe Stock

See BearportPublishing.com for our statement on Generative AI Usage.

Library of Congress Cataloging-in-Publication Data is available at www.loc.gov or upon request from the publisher.

ISBN: 979-8-89232-994-1 (hardcover)
ISBN: 979-8-89577-425-0 (paperback)
ISBN: 979-8-89577-111-2 (ebook)

Copyright © 2026 Bearport Publishing Company. All rights reserved. No part of this publication may be reproduced in whole or in part, stored in any retrieval system, or transmitted in any form or by any means, electronic, mechanical, photocopying, recording, or otherwise, without written permission from the publisher. Bearport Publishing is a division of FlutterBee Education Group.

For more information, write to Bearport Publishing, 3500 American Blvd W, Suite 150, Bloomington, MN 55431.

Contents

Playful Dog 4

Dog Facts 22

Glossary 23

Index 24

Read More 24

Learn More Online 24

About the Author 24

Playful Dog

Woof, woof!

A dog runs fast on four legs.

It has a furry body and a wagging tail.

How did it get this way?

A dog starts its life as a small **embryo**.

It forms after two dogs **mate**.

This embryo grows inside the mother dog's body.

Say embryo like EM-bree-*oh*

7

The embryo grows quickly.

After about four weeks, it starts to form eyes and legs.

A **snout** and paws take shape, too.

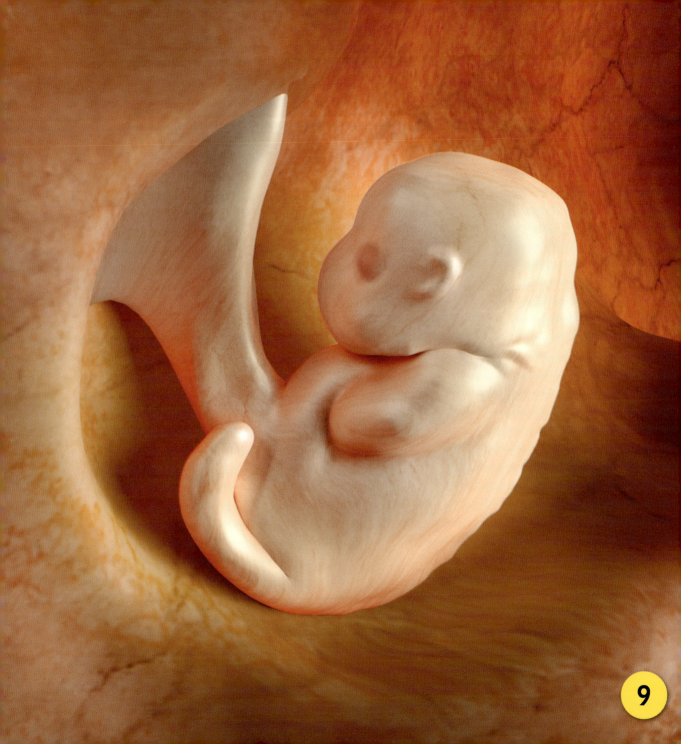

By seven weeks, the baby is covered in fur.

It looks like a small dog.

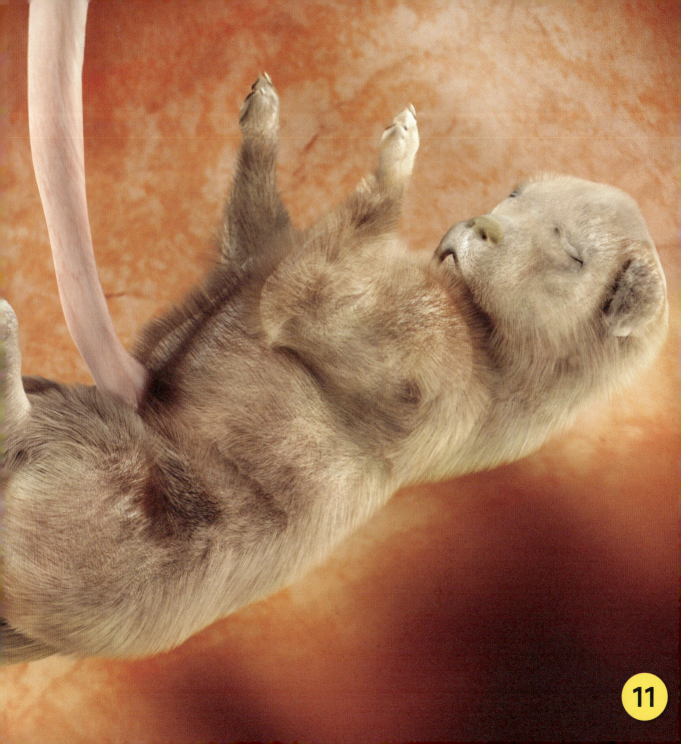

The mother's belly gets big.

There are many puppies growing inside her!

After nine weeks, the mother gives **birth**.

A newborn puppy is very small.

Its eyes and ears are closed.

The pup sniffs to find its mother.

It drinks milk from her body.

15

About two weeks later, the puppy's eyes and ears open.

It can see and hear for the first time!

When it is four weeks old, the puppy begins walking.

At first, its legs are wobbly.

But the little dog becomes stronger.

Soon, it is running.

The puppy grows quickly.

It will be fully grown within a couple of years.

Then, it can have puppies of its own!

Dog Facts

A group of puppies born at the same time is called a litter.

There are more than 300 kinds of dogs. They come in many sizes and colors.

One of the smallest kinds of dogs is the Chihuahua (chih-WAH-wah). One of the largest is the Great Dane.

Glossary

birth when a mother dog has puppies

embryo an animal in the first stage of growth

mate to come together to have young

snout the nose and mouth area of a dog

Index

embryo 6, 8
fur 4, 10
legs 4, 8, 18
litter 22
milk 14
mother 6, 12, 14
snout 8

Read More

Anderhagen, Anna. *Puppies: A First Look (Read About Baby Animals).* Minneapolis: Lerner Publications, 2025.

Sexton, Colleen. *Baby Dogs (Too Cute! Baby Animals).* Minneapolis: Kaleidoscope, 2023.

Learn More Online

1. Go to **FactSurfer.com** or scan the QR code below.
2. Enter "**Dogs Grow**" into the search box.
3. Click on the cover of this book to see a list of websites.

About the Author

Rex Ruby lives in Minnesota with his family. His favorite kind of dog is a golden retriever!

24